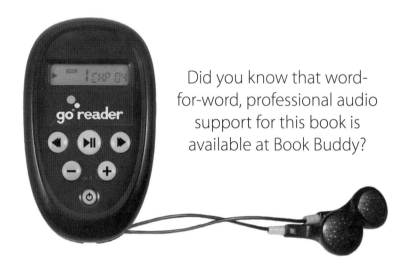

Did you know that word-for-word, professional audio support for this book is available at Book Buddy?

GoReader™ powered by Book Buddy is pre-loaded with word-for-word audio support to build strong readers and achieve Common Core standards.

The corresponding GoReader™ for this book can be found at: http://bookbuddyaudio.com

Or send an email to: info@bookbuddyaudio.com

YES *SHE* DID!

LAW ENFORCEMENT

Yes She Did! Law Enforcement

Scobre Educational
2255 Calle Clara
La Jolla, CA 92037

Scobre Operations & Administration
42982 Osgood Road
Fremont, CA 94539

www.scobre.com
info@scobre.com

Scobre Educational publications may be purchased for educational, business, or sales promotional use.

Cover and layout design by Jana Ramsay
Copyedited by Renae Reed
Some photos by Getty Images

ISBN: 978-161570-936-6 (Soft Cover)
ISBN: 978-1-61570-935-9 (Library Bound)
ISBN: 978-1-61570-933-5 (eBook)

TABLE OF CONTENTS

CHAPTER 1
WOMEN IN TRAINING

Imagine sitting in your classroom when the fire alarm goes off. Only this time, it's not a drill. Everyone runs. But not Melissa Carter and her dog, Josey. When the alarm went off at Union County High School, they raced towards the cause of the alarm. Once they

MAN'S BEST FRIEND

K-9 police dogs, like Josey, are regular members of the team. Like their humans, the dogs are paid a salary—only theirs is paid in food and toys!

4

found the source, they flew through five miles of creeks, woods, and thickets that surround the campus, chasing down the criminals. Melissa is a K-9 handler for the Union County Sheriff's Department in Tennessee, so it was her duty to catch the criminal—and she did. However, until recently, Melissa would not have been allowed to chase him down. In fact, if it hadn't been for a minister from Kansas named Alice Wells, female careers in law enforcement may never have happened at all.

The path to women's equality in law enforcement has been a long and hard one. Though the first women joined the police force in 1910, it took almost 100 more years for them to reach equality. The first women in the police force were not like the women we see on TV and in the movies. They weren't even allowed to carry guns or make arrests.

The first woman police officer, Alice Wells, was sworn into the Los Angeles Police Department on

September 12, 1910. She was given a telephone call box, a police rule book, and the "Policewoman's Badge No. 1." She was not allowed to join her male counterparts in their normal duties. Instead, she supervised skating rinks and dance halls. While her job was not very similar to what policewomen do today, it was nonetheless an important step for women. Thanks to her dedication and hard work, by 1915, 16 other cities had added policewomen to their staff. During her career, Wells travelled throughout the United States and Canada promoting the use of female officers, and fighting for their right to be a regular member of the police force. She was an influential and driving force in getting policewomen the equality they have today.

Although Wells paved the way for women in the police force, it wasn't until 1972, more than 60 years later, that women entered

DID YOU KNOW...

Special Agent Christine Karpoch became the first female firearms instructor in 1978. She also shot the coveted perfect score on the FBI's Practical Pistol Range—only a handful of agents have ever accomplished that.

the other major branch of law enforcement: the Federal Bureau of Investigation. The first two women to enter the FBI were an unusual duo that could not have been more different. Joanne Pierce Misko was formerly a nun in New York, while Susan Roley Malone was a member of the United States Marines. However, their unique backgrounds were just what they needed to succeed.

PROMISE TO PROTECT

Thanks to Alice Wells, we don't see all-male police recruits anymore, like in the picture below. Today, two of every 10 recruits are women.

7

When Misko and Malone entered the FBI Academy in Quantico, Virginia, they were given no special treatment. They were expected to meet the same physical and academic standards as the men. Misko and Malone relied on each other and worked hard for their success. When the other special agent recruits were taking the night off, Misko was helping Malone study, or Malone was helping Misko in the gym. And their hard

RAISING THE BAR

Just like Misko and Malone, women today must pass rigorous physical and mental tests to earn their place in the Federal Bureau of Investigation.

work paid off. In October of 1972, Misko and Malone became the first female special agents in the FBI.

During their time in Quantico and their careers as agents, the FBI never made a big deal about Misko's and Malone's success. According to Malone, "They wanted us to be like any other agent." While this may seem unfair, it was actually beneficial for women. Because women were expected to meet the same standards as men, they, unlike the policewomen, reached equality almost overnight. However, women might never have been given the opportunity to prove their worth in the FBI if women like Malone and Misko hadn't made it possible. Thanks to the work of a minister, a nun, and a marine, many women, such as Jan Fedarcyk and Jennifer Fulford, dedicate their lives to law enforcement careers.

DID YOU KNOW...

A fugitive in Susan Misko's first case tried to refuse arrest because he was too embarassed to be arrested by a woman.

CHAPTER 2
GIRLS WITH GUNS

Law enforcement personnel are people who ensure that others follow the law. The most common type of law enforcement officers are agents. An agent is a detective or investigator for a state, county, or federal government. They are the ones who are on the streets leading investigations and keeping our cities safe. One such agent is Detective Jennifer Fulford-Salvano of the Orange County, Florida Sheriff's Department.

Jennifer Fulford always wanted to be a cop. Her mom was in law enforcement, and growing up she had always been fascinated with TV cop shows. So, after graduating

DID YOU KNOW...

George Washington created the Badge of Military Merit during the American Revolution, as an award to honor the ordinary soldier for extraordinary acts. The Badge of Military Merit has evolved to become the Purple Heart medal given to soldiers and law enforcement officers today.

from the University of South Florida, Jennifer joined the Orange County Sheriff's Office.

Deputy Jennifer Fulford spent her first few years as a policewoman as a general agent. She spent her days doing patrols and running investigations. It was on a routine day like this, after only three years as a policewoman, that her life changed.

In 2004, Jennifer and three other policemen on patrol responded to an emergency call from an eight-year-old boy. He told the dispatcher that there were men with guns in his house, and that they had trapped him and his two sisters in their mini-van in the garage. When Fulford got to the scene,

FIRST RESPONDERS

Patrol officers are responsible for monitoring a certain area. They respond to 911 calls, make arrests, and are usually the first to arrive at the scene of a crime.

11

she quickly entered the garage to get the children to safety. However, before she could get to them, two men emerged from the house firing their weapons right at Fulford. Trapped, and desperate to protect the kids, Fulford fired back. She was struck by 10 bullets, including one that disabled her shooting hand. However, this did not render Fulford helpless. Because she had been through the difficult police training process, she knew just what to do. And she did it.

Fulford received the Purple Heart for her actions. The certificate says, "You transitioned from your dominant hand to your weak hand and continued the battle. Your tremendous courage, focus, and will to survive resulted in one of the suspects being killed, another fatally injured, and a third surrendering without further incident." Fulford saved the kids and brought the criminals to justice.

Jennifer Fulford proved

DID YOU KNOW...

Jennifer Fulford was on the cover of Parade Magazine after she was voted Police Officer of the Year.

that women can be great police officers. When Fulford entered the house, it didn't matter that she was a woman. She relied on her training and responded perfectly in a high-stress situation. However, not all women in law enforcement find themselves in these life-threatening situations. Many, like Ethel and Marlo McGuire, have the training for the situations, but thankfully have never had to use it.

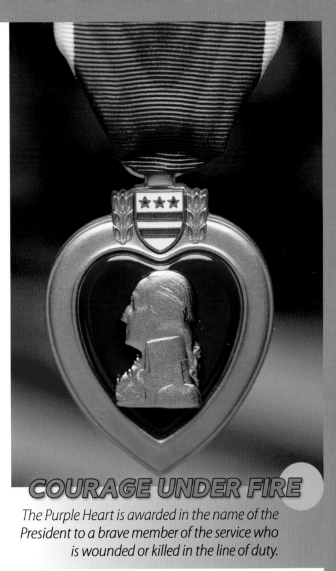

COURAGE UNDER FIRE

The Purple Heart is awarded in the name of the President to a brave member of the service who is wounded or killed in the line of duty.

Ethel and Marlo McGuire represent the minority in the FBI. Not only are they African-American women—they are also the first mother-daughter special agent duo

13

in the history of the FBI. However, being the minority has in no way held Ethel or Marlo back; both women are instrumental members of the FBI.

When Ethel McGuire entered the FBI, she entered an agency where women were still vastly outnumbered. Ethel never saw this as a disadvantage. "Sometimes, it's actually an advantage being a female," said Ethel,

PROTECT AND SERVE

Though less than five percent of policemen and policewomen actually fire their gun during their careers, they are all trained to protect themselves and others in combat if the situation arises.

"because not a lot of people expect us to be in law enforcement. Therefore, we

have an advantage when it comes to investigating cases." Most people don't expect women to be agents, so they don't arouse suspicion when talking to suspects. Many people also feel more comfortable talking with women and are more likely to open up to female agents, allowing them to obtain valuable information. Ethel definitely used her advantage to become the best agent she could be—a trait she passed on to her daughter. "I always admired my mom," said Marlo, "and thought anything she deemed worth doing I should do as well. So after working two summers for the Bureau, I became determined to become an FBI agent." Like her mother, Marlo became a special agent.

Ethel and Marlo are great representations of the positions specials agents can hold in the FBI. Marlo is a field agent in Oakland, California. Her typical day involves conducting investigations, talking to sources, attending to paperwork, gathering evidence, and assisting in the prosecution of cases.

Ethel, on the other hand, moved up from a field agent to a management position. In addition to being the assistant special agent in charge (ASAC), she was the executive manager of the Counterterrorism Branch in Los Angeles. She was responsible for managing six squads with dozens of agents who worked to keep Los Angeles safe. That is an amazing achievement which set the bar very high for women. But one woman, Janice Fedarcyk, showed everyone that, today, there is no bar too high for women to reach.

Janice Fedarcyk entered the FBI in 1987. She started in the Los Angeles division, where she investigated organized crime, drugs, and gang activity. But Janice quickly moved up in the Bureau. By 1996, she was working at the FBI Headquarters, where she coordinated FBI response to domestic and international crises. Janice continued to move up the ranks until, in 2007, she returned to Los Angeles. Only this time, she was there as the special

FOCUS OF THE FORCE

The FBI's motto is Fidelity, Bravery, and Integrity. Or, to put it shortly, "FBI."

agent in charge (SAC)—the boss. But Janice was still not done advancing.

In 2010, Janice Fedarcyk became the highest-ranked woman in law enforcement. She was named the assistant director in charge (ADIC) of New York, the largest field office in the country. Janice was responsible for the performance of more than 1,000 agents. Though Janice retired after only two years in New York, she proved that women are just as capable of leading as men. When

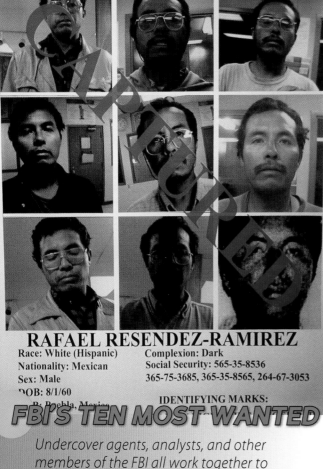
FBI'S TEN MOST WANTED

Undercover agents, analysts, and other members of the FBI all work together to capture the FBI's most-wanted criminals.

asked about her accomplishments, Janice said, "I never viewed myself as a female agent. I was a special agent of the FBI." Though gender was not Janice's focus, she nonetheless opened countless doors for women.

Not all women in law enforcement are restricted to wielding guns or taking up management positions. Many, including Candice DeLong and Stephanie Benitez, use their talents to take up special skills within their agent duties.

CHAPTER 3
FACING FEARS

There's much more to being an agent than investigating leads and making arrests; agents can choose to pursue dozens of other career paths. By utilizing their special talents, agents can be accountants, analysts, undercover agents, or intelligence personnel—just to name a few. Some agents, like Stephanie Benitez, have extremely unique specialties within the agency.

Stephanie is a special agent of the FBI who has a dangerously exciting job within the Bureau. Stephanie is an active member of USERT: The FBI's Underwater Search and Evidence Recovery Team. The FBI's USERT is one of the most elite search and recovery

DID YOU KNOW...

USERT members search to recover evidence or work on humanitarian missions. They are not a tactical team, like the Navy SEALs.

teams in the world. It is comprised of only 50 members. The members must be prepared to go anywhere in the world at a moment's notice. The training is rigorous because they must be prepared for any situation.

In 2007, the I-35W Mississippi River Bridge collapsed in Minneapolis, Minnesota. Dozens of cars dropped into the freezing river, killing 13 people and injuring more than 100. Immediate help came to pull victims out of the water, but that wasn't the end. For USERT, it was just the beginning.

In situations like this, someone now needs to get in the river and pull out the people and vehicles that are trapped under the fallen bridge. Someone has to dive down in dark, freezing water through dangerous rubble looking for the bodies. Someone has to find clues in the debris under water to determine what happened. That someone is Stephanie; this is the type of situation

DID YOU KNOW...

Diving with a helmet and other gear, the total weight of the equipment that a USERT diver wears can exceed 100 pounds.

that Stephanie is faced with as a USERT diver.

Stephanie and other USERT divers have advanced training for their job. Because they work underwater in dark, difficult environments, they must know how to dive in strong currents more than 100 feet below the surface without being able to see. In addition, they are trained to use many high-tech tools like sonar and metal detectors to find objects and clues. They also use

DIVING DEEP

USERT divers must be prepared to work in all kinds of dangerous, extreme environments.

Remotely Operated Vehicles, like this one, are used to perform deep-water search and recovery missions, because they can reach depths unhealthy for humans.

remotely operated vehicles (ROVs), and underwater scooters to move efficiently underwater so they can stay down longer to con-duct their investigation. While underwater, USERT members take photographs, diagram and survey scenes, recover DNA, and find clues. With their high-tech equipment, they can even find a bullet buried more than a foot down in the silt!

Being a member of such an elite team is no small task for a woman. Stephanie must be as physically and mentally prepared as the men on the squad. But that didn't stop Stephanie. She worked hard to get where she is today, as have other women who chose to serve in law enforcement. One such woman is Candice DeLong, a retired FBI profiler who found success long before TV shows like "Criminal Minds" and "CSI: Crime Scene Investigation" made profiling something cool to talk about.

Candice DeLong was raised with three brothers in the 1950s. Like most girls at that time, Candice believed that her options were limited. However, her father didn't agree, so he pushed her to go to college, where she got her degree as a nurse. When she graduated, Candice was hired at Northwestern Memorial Hospital outside of Chicago as a psychiatric nurse. She dealt with people that everybody else avoided—criminals. It was the first time she was acquainted with people who had done horrible crimes. However, while others were hesitant to interact with violent patients, Candice was compelled

to work with them. "I wanted to know what was going on in their minds, hearts, and lives to make them do the horrible things they'd done," she said. Over her eight years as a psychiatric nurse, Candice became an expert on the minds of criminals. It was for this reason that the FBI offered Candice a job. In 1980, Candice hung up her scrubs and became an FBI profiler.

An FBI profiler is a special agent who analyzes criminal cases in order to figure out what type of person usually commits a specific type of crime. Profilers understand what makes criminals tick, and use that knowledge to help catch the bad guy. Once the criminal is caught, the profiler then interviews them to gain insight into the motives and patterns of other criminals.

When Candice became a profiler, she set three goals for herself: She wanted to be involved with a high-profile national criminal, to apprehend a serial killer, and to rescue a kidnap victim. Over the course of her 20-year career, Candice did all three.

In 1995, Candice was one of three hand-picked FBI agents to find the "Una-bomber", Ted Kaczynski. Ted Kaczynski had sent 16 bombs to various targets, killing three people and injuring 23 more. Candice and two other agents

BEHIND BARS

Ted Kaczynski, the "Unabomber," sent 16 bombs to various locations around the United States before being apprehended by Candice DeLong.

tracked the Unabomber to a remote wilderness cabin in Montana, where he was later arrested. However, while the Unabomber case gave Candice world-wide attention and fulfilled two of her three goals, it was not her most defining moment. It was as a member of the San Francisco bureau's Child Abduction Task Force that Candice had the greatest day of her career.

A nine-year-old boy had been kidnapped and his

LIFE AFTER PROFILING

Candice DeLong is the host of the Investigation Discovery programs Deadly Women *and* Facing Evil with Candice DeLong.

parents were desperate to find him. Candice and several other agents worked tirelessly to help the parents find their son. They knew that most kidnapping victims are never found, and they were determined to make sure that this boy wasn't one of them. Their determination paid off. Through their investigation, Candice and her team learned that the boy and his abductor were on a train to San Diego. They used their skills to rescue the boy and arrest the criminal. Candice flew home with the boy, and took him home to his family. As he was running to the arms of his parents, he stopped and said, "Thank you, Agent Candy, for saving me." It brought tears to Candice's eyes, and went down as the best day of her career.

Many women who hear Candice's story, and the stories of other law enforcement women, decide to join because they want to make a difference as well. One such woman is Shanon Demarest.

New recruits for law enforcement have more women among the ranks every year.

Shanon had a dream of becoming a policewoman. But when the time came to apply to the police academy, Shanon found out that she was pregnant. She initially thought that her dream was lost. But she was determined and did

STOP THE UNSTOPPABLE

SWAT Teams are called in to deal with dangerous stand-offs, such as undercover, high-risk, and hostage situations.

not give up. She worked two jobs and moved in with her parents so that she could attend the police academy. And when the SWAT team told her that they had never had a female on the squad, she fought to do that, too.

The Special Weapons and Tactics team, or SWAT, is made up of elite officers who are responsible for resolving high-risk situations. Though the team was open to both genders, no female had ever passed the difficult test for the Polk County Sheriff's Office. But Shanon knew that she could.

The SWAT team tryouts have three phases. Candidates must pass all of the tasks in the first two phases to move on to phase three. Phases one and two include many physical challenges such as a 50-yard timed run in full gear carrying

The SWAT team's standards are set so high that the US Army enlists their help training army reservists.

a 50-pound battering ram, jumping a 6-foot fence in full gear, accurately firing a gun, and dragging the heaviest member of the team (who might weigh over 300 pounds) out of a dangerous situation. Shanon was the first female at the Polk County Sheriff's Office to pass phases one and two. So Shanon, along with 10 male classmates, moved on to phase three.

The final phase of the SWAT trial is a 64-hour course. Shanon spent the first three days running, doing tactical drills, and taking physical endurance tests. By the end of the third day, Shanon was exhausted. But she knew that she only had to complete one more day to make history—to be the first female SWAT member.

On the last day of the final phase, Shanon had to negotiate the SWAT obstacle course, which consisted of 20 obstacles. While she ran the course, Shanon was surrounded by sirens blaring and instructors screaming at her. This was done to make sure that she had the ability to focus in any situation. And she did.

On January 13th, 2012, Shanon Demarest was welcomed as the first female SWAT member of the Polk County Sheriff's Office in Lake Wales, Florida. Demarest was proud of her accomplishment, and the fact that she passed the same physical standards as men. "Because if I made the team," Shanon said, "the guys I'm backing up, I want them to have faith in me. I don't want them to think 'I got the girl behind me.'"

Shanon, Candice, and Stephanie prove that females can be highly successful as special agents. But there are also many women who choose to make an impact in law enforcement outside of the agencies. As Jackie Lacey can attest, there are many other fulfilling positions in law enforcement.

CHAPTER 4
THE SCALES OF JUSTICE

Once the agents arrest a criminal, the job of law enforcement is not done. The criminal is passed on to the court system, where they are proven to be either guilty or not guilty. The person who is accused of the crime is defended by a lawyer, while the government (law enforcement) is represented by a prosecutor. A prosecutor is a lawyer who works with the government in criminal cases. As with most jobs, prosecutors can move

LAYING DOWN THE LAW

The job of law enforcement is not done until the criminal is brought in front of a court.

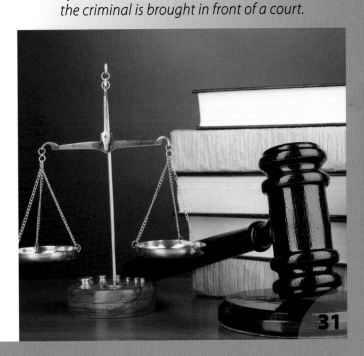

Jackie Lacey is the Los Angeles District Attorney. In 2009, she was named one of the Top 100 Women Litigators in the United States.

up in their career, taking on greater responsibilities and prestige. The highest office for prosecutors is the district attorney. In December of 2012, Los Angeles County got a new district attorney: Jackie Lacey.

Jackie Lacey was born and raised in Los Angeles. Her father was a cleaning employee, and her mother worked in a garment factory. No one in her family had gone to college—her mom hadn't even graduated from high school. Yet humble beginnings did not stop Jackie from pursuing her goals.

After graduating from college, and then from the University of Southern California Gould School of Law in 1982, Lacey joined the Los Angeles County District

Attorney's Office. During her time as a prosecutor, Lacey tried (prosecuted) 60 felony cases, including 11 murder cases. She even made national news after winning one of her cases.

Jackie's big case, People v. Rojas, was the first case of a race-motivated hate crime in Los Angeles. When we think of Nazis and racism, we usually think of something that happened in the past. However, Lacey proved that three men—Rojas, Bryant, and Colwell—beat an older African-American man to death because they were trying to join a Nazi gang. The men, thanks to the work of special agents and Jackie Lacey, were all found guilty and put in jail.

As a prosecutor, Lacey was just as awesome as the lawyers you see on television who put the bad guys in jail. Now, as a district attorney, she's even more impressive. District Attorney Lacey has a huge job. She oversees

DID YOU KNOW...

Jackie Lacey established the Animal Cruelty Prosecution Program to help protect animals from violence and abuse.

Judges are considered members of law enforcement, too.

roughly 1,000 lawyers, 300 investigators, and more than 800 support staff employees. She reviews every major case that comes into the office, and works hard to make sure that the office runs smoothly.

Jackie Lacey is the first female, and the first African American to serve as Los Angeles County District Attorney. When she retires, her picture will be placed next to the pictures of 160 years' worth of white males who held the position before her. However, Lacey was definitely not hired for her physical appearance. In an interview, Lacey said, "I'm the most qualified person. I've worked my butt off. If you don't know what I look like and you looked at whose résumé had the most relevant experience, it would hands-down be my résumé."

However, Lacey has not forgotten her past. Amidst her busy schedule, Lacey frequently gives back to her community. On a weekly basis, Lacey meets with the students of Lorena Street Elementary School. During her meetings, she talks with the kids about her own background and how hard she worked to get where she is today. She also discusses with them the consequences of stealing, doing drugs, and other crimes. She hopes that by talking to the kids now, she can keep them from visiting someone

35

like Kelly Grice when they get older.

Kelly Grice is a probation officer. She is responsible for supervising people who are out of jail so that the community stays safe. Probation officers are typically men, because many people worry that females won't be able to handle the stresses of the job. However, women like Kelly are proving those stereotypes wrong.

If you saw Kelly Grice on the street, you would never believe that she dealt with criminals

SOCIETY'S SAFETY NET

Probation officers help convicts with their transition out of jail and back into society.

and past-criminals on a daily basis. She is small and cute, with the world's biggest

smile. However, you shouldn't let her outer appearance deceive you. Not only is she a probation officer—she's a good one.

Probation officers have a lot of responsibility. They must decide whether someone needs to go back to jail, or if they are able stay out and do the right thing. As Kelly points out, it's a strange job because when it goes right, nothing happens. However, if they make the wrong call and someone commits another crime, the probation officer gets blamed.

That being said, Kelly wouldn't change her job for the world. "It's the kind of job that, at the end of the week, I'll always have the sense of having actually achieved something," she said. Every day, Kelly works to keep her community safe.

CHAPTER 5
THE FEMALE FORCE

Women have proven that they have what it takes to succeed in law enforcement. Today, women have the same responsibilities and duties as their male counterparts. And though they have yet to reach the highest levels of power, women like Janice Fedarcyk are working hard to raise the ceiling and get there.

Barbara Boxer, a United States Senator from California, stated, "Law enforcement officers are never 'off duty.' They are dedicated public servants who are sworn to protect public safety at any time and place that the peace is threatened." The women in law enforcement are no exception.

The women in this book, along with thousands

DID YOU KNOW...

Roughly 17 percent of police officers today are women.

of others, are proving once again that the role of women in traditionally male professions is changing. Women in law enforcement have a hard job because their profession is associated with power and strength. But, as Shanon Demarest has shown us, they can do it. To succeed in law

POSITIONS OF POWER

Before earning a place in the Senate, Barbara Boxer worked as a journalist for the Pacific Sun, a weekly newspaper.

enforcement, women must be dedicated and willing to put the public ahead of themselves.

Whether you're a profiler like Candice DeLong, a probation officer like Kelly Grice, or anything in between, there is a valuable place in law enforcement for you.

Women in law enforcement work tirelessly to make the world a safer place for the rest of us. Thanks to the work of many brave women who showed the world that they are valuable members of this elite group, the possibilities for women in law enforcement are endless.

PROUD TO PROTECT

Women in law enforcement have not only dedicated their lives to protecting the public, they have also proved that women are capable of upholding the law and serving their country.

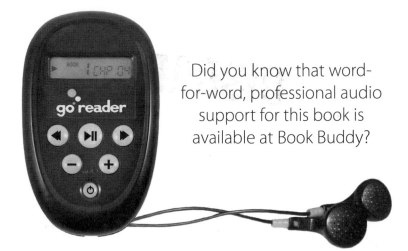

Did you know that word-for-word, professional audio support for this book is available at Book Buddy?

GoReader™ powered by Book Buddy is pre-loaded with word-for-word audio support to build strong readers and achieve Common Core standards.

The corresponding GoReader™ for this book can be found at: http://bookbuddyaudio.com

Or send an email to: info@bookbuddyaudio.com